D0515777

394.2
FRA

Fradin, Dennis B.   73006

Halloween

$18.42

DATE DUE	BORROWER'S NAME	ROOM NO.

Halloween

Dennis Brindell Fradin

—Best Holiday Books—

Enslow Publishers, Inc.

44 Fadem Road	PO Box 38
Box 699	Aldershot
Springfield, NJ 07081	Hants GU12 6BP
USA	UK

> For my wonderful son, Michael Louis Fradin

Library of Congress Cataloging-in-Publication Data

Fradin, Dennis B.
Halloween / by Dennis Brindell Fradin.
   p. cm.—(Best holiday books)
     Includes index.
     Summary: Describes the history behind Halloween and the various ways it is
celebrated.
     ISBN 0-89490-234-2
     1. Halloween—Juvenile literature. {1. Halloween.} I. Title. II. Series: Fradin,
Dennis B. Best holiday books.
GT4965.F73 1990
394.2'683—dc20   89-7681
                            CIP
                            AC

Printed in the United States of America

10 9 8 7 6 5

Illustration Credits:
Cameramann International, Ltd.: pp. 7, 9, 24, 25, 28, 32, 36, 37, 40; Tom Dunnington:
pp. 11, 22, 27, 30; Photos by Mary Emmer: pp. 8, 41; Historical Pictures Service,
Chicago: pp. 13, 15, 18; Library of Congress: pp. 34, 39; Norma Morrison: p. 4; U.S.
Committee for UNICEF/National UNICEF Day: p. 44.

Cover Illustration by Charlott Nathan

Contents

Children carving a pumpkin for Halloween

A Spooky (But Fun) Day

It happens every fall. Paper ghosts and witches go up on schoolroom walls. Stores sell pumpkins. Children talk about what they will "be for Halloween."

In late October, families carve their pumpkins. Since Halloween is supposed to be a spooky day, many people carve scary pumpkin faces. But some people carve happy or funny faces into their pumpkins. They place the pumpkins in windows or on doorsteps.

Meanwhile, Halloween costumes must be gotten ready. Some parents help their children make their costumes. Others buy the costumes in stores. Ghost, witch, and cat costumes are popular with many children. So are princess and bunny costumes.

Finally, October 31 arrives. It is Halloween! Schools have parades of children in costume. Many classes have Halloween parties. After school, children put on their costumes again. They go from door to door saying, "Trick or treat." Most people give them candy.

Many communities hold special Halloween events. Pumpkin contests are held in some places. Prizes are given for the scariest or best-looking pumpkins. "Haunted houses" for children are also popular. A "haunted house" may have paper ghosts hanging from the ceiling. Scary music may be playing in the background. Ghost stories may be told at the "haunted house." And there may be a "fortune-teller" who pretends to know the children's future. Before leaving the "haunted house," the children may get candy.

Millions of teenagers and adults enjoy Halloween, too. High schools and colleges hold Halloween dances. Some adults hold Halloween parties in their homes.

The ghost, the witch, and the black cat are trick-or-treating. Does the woman seem scared of them?

An entry in the Sycamore, Illinois, pumpkin festival that is held each Halloween

Some parents read their children scary stories on Halloween.

The Roots of Halloween

In the fall the nights get longer. The weather turns colder. Leaves fall from trees, and plants die. For these reasons, fall has long been thought of as a time of death.

Long ago, many people believed that on certain fall nights dead spirits came back to earth. This idea was held by the Celts, a European people who lived in England, Scotland, Wales, Ireland, and France. Over 2,000 years ago, the Celts held a festival that was probably the start of our Halloween.

The Celts' festival was held on October 31. It was called Samhain, after the Celts' lord of the dead. Samhain was thought to send ghosts

The Celts built fires to scare away ghosts.

to earth on the night of October 31. When angry, Samhain could send many evil ghosts. The Celts built fires on hilltops to scare off the ghosts. They also scared the ghosts away by wearing costumes made of animal heads and skins.

There was a way to keep Samhain happy. That was to sacrifice (kill) animals and people in his name. Celtic priests called Druids burned live animals during Samhain's festival. They also burned human enemies. If Samhain was pleased, he supposedly gave people hints about the future. Samhain was thought to hide the clues in the burned bodies of the animals and people. The Druids studied these remains. They told the future based on what they saw.

Traces of the Samhain festival remain in our Halloween customs. Ghosts still roam about on October 31. Only today they are children under sheets. People still wear costumes on Halloween. Only now they are cloth and plastic instead of animal heads and skins.

Fortune-telling is still done, but just for fun. Even Halloween's colors—orange and black— may have come from the Samhain festival. It was a time when orange flames lit up the black night.

Celts listening to a Druid priest

The Romans Add
to the Tradition

The Romans were a mighty people of ancient times. At first they lived in Rome, in what is now Italy. Later they conquered many other lands. Near the time of Christ's birth, the Romans conquered the Celts. They changed the way of life for people in England, France, and other Celtic lands.

Each fall the Romans honored the dead with a festival. It was called the Feralia. It came in late October, about the time of Samhain. Little is known about the Feralia. Near that time of the year the Romans also had a harvest festival. It honored Pomona, their goddess of fruit trees. Pomona was sometimes shown wearing a crown of apples. She was nicknamed the Apple Queen.

To thank Pomona for fruits, the Romans set out apples and nuts for her. They also ate apples and nuts. And they ran races and played games.

These Roman customs blended with the Celts' Samhain customs. As a result, the October 31 holiday became less concerned with killing. And apples and nuts became early Halloween foods.

Pomona, the Roman goddess of fruit trees

Today, apples and nuts are served at many Halloween parties. "Bobbing for apples" is also popular at Halloween parties. A number of apples are placed in a tub of water. Using only their teeth, the contestants try to grab the apples. The one who sinks his or her teeth into an apple first wins a prize.

All Hallows'
Even = Halloween

About 2,000 years ago, Jesus Christ was born. He founded a new religion. It was named Christianity, after Jesus Christ.

After Christ's death, Christianity spread through Europe. By 600 A.D. (600 years after Christ's birth), many Celts had become Christians. Christian priests disliked the old Celtic holidays. They wanted the Celts to honor Christian holidays instead. But the Celts would not give up their old holidays.

The Christian priests found a way to solve this problem. They made Christian holidays on the same days as old Celtic holidays. They wanted the Christian holidays to slowly replace the Celtic ones.

This Celtic cross was made many hundreds of years ago after the Irish people had become Christians.

In 609 or 610 A.D., the Christians created a new holiday. It was called All Hallows' Day (today All Saints' Day). It honored holy people called saints, many of whom had died for their religion.

At first All Hallows' Day was held in May. But in the 800s A.D., it was moved to November 1. Christian leaders wanted All Saints' Day to replace Samhain.

The night before All Hallows' Day was called All Hallows' Even. This means "All Saints' Evening." After a while, people left off "All" and called it "Hallow Even." But they said "Hallow Even" so fast that it became "Halloween."

Roman ideas had already changed the October 31 festival. Christian ideas changed it much more. Samhain, the lord of the dead, lost importance. The devil replaced him in people's minds. Also called Satan, the devil is the evil ruler of the Christians' hell.

Europe's Middle Ages lasted from the 400s A.D. to the 1500s A.D. During the Middle Ages, many Europeans thought that the devil came up to earth on Halloween. The devil was also thought to send evil spirits up from hell on that night. People had to be careful on the night of October 31. Otherwise spirits might harm them. The devil might even take their souls.

People thought there were magic ways to keep the devil and his spirits away. People in Scotland thought that the rowan tree (or European mountain ash) drove off evil spirits. They wore twigs of this tree for protection on Halloween. They also made cakes for Halloween spirits. They hoped the spirits would be grateful for these treats and leave people alone.

In Wales and some other places people were afraid to sneeze on Halloween. They thought a sneeze shot the soul out of the body for a second. The devil could take the soul to hell in that time. Quickly saying "God bless you" protected the loose soul from the devil. That may be why people say "God bless you" to sneezers today.

Witches and Black Cats

During the Middle Ages and through the 1700s, most Europeans believed in witches. Supposedly witches sold their souls to the devil. In return, the devil gave them wealth and magic powers. Most witches were thought to be cruel. They were believed to make their enemies sick and ruin their crops. Most of the accused witches were women, but some were men.

People thought there were ways to "prove" that someone was a witch. Witches supposedly appeared in people's dreams. Someone would say: "I dreamed that so-and-so is a witch." Soon half the town might be calling the person a witch.

People once believed that witches could fly.

It was also thought that witches had odd moles and birthmarks. Accused witches were tied up. They were examined to see if they had strange marks on their bodies.

From the late 1500s to the late 1700s, over a quarter of a million so-called witches were killed in Europe. Most were women. Many were tortured before being put to death.

Black cats also suffered from the witch scare. It was widely thought that black cats were witches' special pets. Some people even thought that witches could turn into black cats. Many thousands of black cats were killed as a result.

Halloween was considered a special night for witches. It was thought that they flew through the air to a meeting with the devil on Halloween. And witches were supposedly extra dangerous on that night. To this day, witches and black cats are a big part of Halloween. They appear in Halloween stories and artwork. And many little witches and black cats trick-or-treat on Halloween!

Gizmo, the author's black cat, with Mikey, the author's son. It was once thought that black cats were witches' pets.

A schoolgirl making a Halloween witch for an art project

Halloween
Jack-o'-lanterns

Each year, millions of people carve Halloween pumpkins. The carved pumpkins are nicknamed "jack-o'-lanterns." The custom of carving Halloween jack-o'-lanterns began long ago in Ireland and Scotland. But when the custom began, people in those lands did not have pumpkins. (They are thought to have grown first in North America.) The people in Ireland and Scotland carved jack-o'-lanterns out of turnips.

An Irish story told how jack-o'-lanterns got their name. Long ago, the story began, a man named Jack met the devil on a road. Jack had been very selfish. He knew the devil would take

Jack with the devil

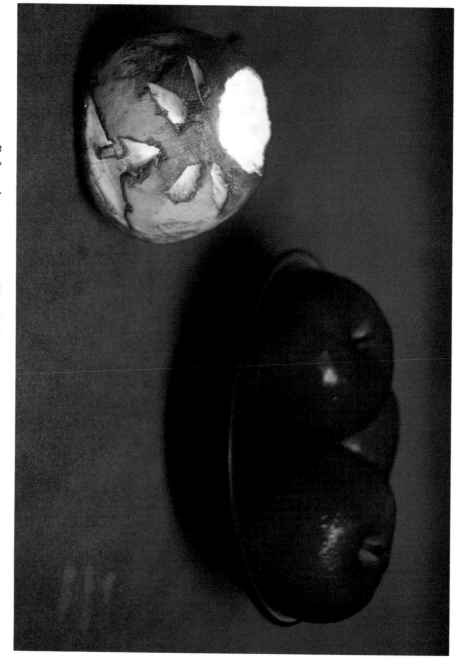

Before there were pumpkins in Ireland, people carved turnips.

his soul—unless he could fool him. As they passed an apple tree, Jack had an idea. He asked for an apple before going to hell.

The devil climbed the tree to get the apple. As he did so, Jack carved a cross on the tree with his knife. The devil was scared to come down past the cross, which is a symbol of Christianity's good power. Jack helped the devil down—but only after he promised to leave Jack's soul alone.

Jack soon died. He could not enter heaven because he had been so bad. Needing a place to go, Jack tried to enter hell. But the devil kept his promise and would not let him in. The devil said that Jack must return to earth. When Jack cried that he could not find his way in the dark, the devil threw him a hot coal. Jack carved a turnip and placed the glowing coal inside it. Ever since, Jack has wandered the earth with his turnip lantern.

Turnips with lighted candles inside them became known as "jack-o'-lanterns" after Jack.

Jack wandering the earth with his turnip lantern

People in Ireland and Scotland carved ugly faces on their jack-o'-lanterns. They placed the glowing jack-o'-lanterns outside their homes on Halloween. They thought that the ugly, glowing faces scared evil Halloween spirits. After Europeans reached America, pumpkins were used as jack-o'-lanterns.

These children may not think of the meaning of the words "Trick or treat" as they go from door to door.

Halloween Comes to America

England built its first permanent town in America in 1607. Between 1607 and 1733, England founded or took over 13 colonies in what is now the United States. English people were the main settlers of the 13 American colonies.

The English did little about Halloween in colonial America. Halloween was not celebrated much here until long after the United States freed itself from England in 1776. During the 1800s, many thousands of people came to the United States from Ireland and Scotland. They were the ones who made Halloween popular in the United States.

Halloween changed in the new country. The American Indians had taught the settlers to grow pumpkins. Pumpkins grow big enough to carve easily. And they are orange—a Halloween color. Irish and Scottish settlers began carving pumpkin jack-o'-lanterns in the United States.

This magazine illustration from 1867 shows a pumpkin with a scary face.

Irish people also helped start "trick-or-treating" in America. Long ago in Ireland, people went from house to house asking for food and money on Halloween. Tricks were played on those who didn't give these treats. Fences were removed. Small fires were set.

Irish children went from house to house after coming to America, too. Children of other backgrounds joined them. Many people gave the children apples and sweets. Those who didn't give treats might find their garbage on their roof the next morning.

Saying the words "Trick or treat" didn't become popular until about 1940. That was about when the custom of going from house to house for candy started to become very popular in the United States. Have you ever thought about the meaning of the words "Trick or treat"? You are really threatening to play a trick if you don't get a treat!

This boy is putting up a pumpkin-man decoration made in school.

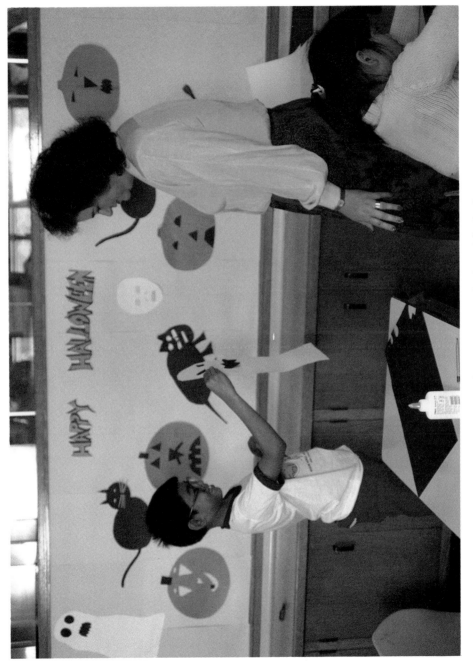

Putting up a Halloween bulletin board is fun!

Halloween Today

Today, Halloween is celebrated mainly in English-speaking nations. It is most popular in the United States. People in Ireland, Canada, Scotland, and England also celebrate Halloween.

Halloween has changed a lot over the years. Yet most of our Halloween customs have very old sources. The next time you hear a scary Halloween story, remember how ancient people greatly feared the coming of fall. As you put on your Halloween costume, think of how the Celts wore animal heads and skins to scare evil spirits. While your Halloween pumpkin is being carved, remember Jack's turnip jack-o'-lantern. And as you trick-or-treat, remember how people in Ireland asked for food and money on long-ago Halloweens.

Children have enjoyed carving pumpkins or watching their parents carve
pumpkins for many years. This photograph was taken in 1917.

Halloween costumes are a little like the Celts' animal heads and skins.

Senior citizens in a nursing home made these pumpkin dolls.

A new kind of trick-or-treating began in the United States in 1950. It is called "trick-or-treating for UNICEF." UNICEF (the United Nations Children's Fund) helps get food and medicine to children in poor countries. Children who "trick-or-treat for UNICEF" go from door to door on Halloween asking people to give money to UNICEF. At the same time, they may trick-or-treat for candy for themselves.

Since 1967, Halloween has been National UNICEF Day. Besides trick-or-treating, many young people hold dances and parties to raise money for UNICEF. By the late 1980s, about 3 million people in the United States were involved in raising money for UNICEF each Halloween.

To learn about "trick-or-treating for UNICEF" and other UNICEF Halloween programs, write:

Group Programs
U.S. Committee for UNICEF
331 E. 38th St.
New York, NY 10016

Halloween was once a day for fear and cruelty. People were terrified of ghosts and spirits on that day. They mistreated "witches" and black cats. They played tricks on those who did not give them treats. With "trick-or-treat for UNICEF" it has become a day when people can have fun while helping others. Can you think of a better way to celebrate Halloween?

Children "trick-or-treating for UNICEF"

Glossary

---

colony—a settlement built by a country beyond its borders

cruelty—meanness

custom—a way of doing things that people teach their children

devil—the evil ruler of the Christians' hell

evil—cruel and harmful

fortune-teller—someone who claims to know the future

jack-o'-lantern—a lantern made of a pumpkin or another plant and carved to look like a face

million—a thousand thousand (1,000,000)

permanent—lasting

sacrifice—this can mean to kill living things in a religious ceremony

saint—a very holy person

terrified—very scared

thousand—ten hundred (1,000)

torture—to badly hurt someone on purpose

trick-or-treating—the custom of going from place to place and asking for Halloween treats

witches—people who supposedly sold their souls to the devil

Index

A All Hallows' Day, 18-19
America. *See* United States.
American Indians, 34
apples, 14, 15, 16, 29, 35

B black cats, 23, 43

C Canada, 38
candy, 6, 35, 42
Celts, 10, 14, 15, 17, 38
Christ, 14, 17
Christians, 17-18, 19
costumes, 5-6, 12, 38

D devil, 19-20, 21, 26, 29
Druids, 12

E England, 10, 14, 33, 38

F Feralia, 14
France, 10, 14

G ghosts, 5, 6, 10, 12, 43

H "haunted houses," 6